SCARY SHARKS

Camilla de la Bédoyère

QEB Publishing

This edition published by Scholastic Inc., 557 Broadway,
New York, NY 10012 by arrangement with QEB Publishing, Inc.

Scholastic and associated logos are trademarks and/or registered
trademarks of Scholastic Inc.

Distributed by:
Scholastic Canada Ltd., Markham, Ontario
Scholastic Australia Pty. Ltd, Gosford NSW
Scholastic New Zealand Ltd., Greenmount, Auckland
Grolier International, Inc., Makati City, Philippines

Created for QEB Publishing by Tall Tree Ltd
www.talltreebooks.co.uk
Editors: Jon Richards and Rob Colson
Designer: Jonathan Vipond
Illustration pp18–19:
Mick Posen/www.the-art-agency.co.uk

Copyright © 2012 QEB Publishing, Inc.

Published in the United States by
QEB Publishing, Inc.
3 Wrigley, Suite A
Irvine, CA 92618

10 9 8 7 6 5 4 3 2 1

A CIP record for this book is available from the
Library of Congress.

ISBN: 978-0-545-48282-0

Printed in Shenzhen City, China

Picture credits
(t=top, b=bottom, l=left, r=right, c=center, fc=front cover,
bc=back cover)
Alamy 28-29 Stephen Frink Collection, 30b WaterFrame;
FLPA 16 Mike Parry/Minden Pictures, 20-21 Norbert Wu/
Minden Pictures, 21b Reinhard Dirscherl, 22-23 Norbert
Wu/Minden Pictures, 27t D P Wilson; **Getty** 1 Stuart
Westmorland, 5b Mark Conlin, 6-7 Doug Perrine; **Nature
Picture Library** 2-3 Alex Mustard, 7b Doug Perrine,
8-9 Doug Perrine, 9t Dan Burton, 14b Alan James,
23t Alex Hyde, 24-25 Alex Mustard, 25t David Fleetham,
26-27 Doug Perrine, 30-31 Jeff Rotman; **Photolibrary**
fc; **NHPA** 4b, 4-5t Burt Jones and Maurine Shimlock,
12b, 33b Charles Hood, 12-13t Charles Hood, 15t Charles
Hood, 17t Oceans Image/Photoshot/Saul Gonor;
Shutterstock bctl, bctr, bcb Ian Scott, 2-3, 4-5, 10-11,
12-13, 14-15, 32-33, 34 EpicStockMedia; **SPL** 10t Andy
Murch, Visuals Unlimited, Inc., 11t Andy Murch/Visuals
Unlimited, Inc., 11b Georgette Douwma, 15b Gerald and
Buff Corsi, Visuals Unlimited, Inc., 17b Andy Murch/
Visuals Unlimited, Inc., 20b Geoff Kidd.

Website information is correct at time of going to press.
However, the publishers cannot accept liability for any
information or links found on any Internet sites,
including third-party websites.

Words in **bold** are explained in the Glossary on page 32.

HOW **SCARY?**

Look out for this rating. It will tell you how scary and dangerous each shark is!

1 – a bit scary

2 – pretty scary

3 – scary

4 – QUICK! SWIM AWAY!

5 – AAAARGH! TOO LATE!

CONTENTS

SUPER PREDATORS 4

BULL SHARK 6

GRAY REEF SHARK 8

ON THE MOVE 10

HAMMERHEAD SHARK... 12

BASKING SHARK 14

GREAT WHITE SHARK.. 16

GREAT WHITE SHARK 18

TIGER SHARK 20

SKELETONS AND SCALES 22

LEMON SHARK 24

EGGS AND PUPS... 26

LONGNOSE SAWSHARK 28

SHARKS AND PEOPLE 30

GLOSSARY 32

TAKING IT FURTHER 33

INDEX 34

Actual size!

Check out this lemon shark on page 24

SUPER PREDATORS

A giant fish swims through the ocean, and its body casts a dark shadow on the seabed below. With its huge teeth, super speed, and cold, dead eyes, this shark is one of the world's most impressive **predators**.

Most sharks are long and thin, but they come in all shapes and sizes. The largest fish in the world is the mighty whale shark. It is harmless to people because it feeds on tiny animals called **plankton**.

Whale sharks are the giants of the ocean and grow to about 36 feet (11 meters) in length.

Frilled sharks have long, thin bodies and live deep underwater.

KILLER FACT

Sharks have been around for 400 million years, and had few predators—until humans began to hunt them.

All sharks are fish. They eat other animals, such as fish and squid. Sometimes, sharks mistake humans for food and attack them. Most sharks are afraid of humans and try to avoid them. However, there are some sharks that are more aggressive.

This blue shark has a pointed nose, or snout, and large eyes so that it can see well in deep water.

BULL SHARK

This broad, strong shark is known for its aggressive nature. Bull sharks are described as "short-tempered," which means they are always ready for a fight!

Bull sharks usually live and hunt on their own.

Almost all sharks live in seas and oceans, where the water is salty. Bull sharks are more adaptable. They live in shallow coastal waters, but they also swim up rivers, and have even been found in **freshwater** lakes. Spotting a bull shark can be difficult, because they often swim in cloudy water.

KILLER FACT

Some experts believe that the bull shark is the deadliest shark in the world.

SHARK BITES

Length: Up to 11 ft (340 cm)

Habitat: Coasts, rivers, and bays

Where: Warm tropical waters

Weapons: Very aggressive, rapid acceleration, razor-sharp teeth

Lateral line

Sensitive Senses

Bull sharks have poor eyesight. Instead, they rely on a superb sense of smell. Like other sharks, they have a sensitive line that runs along their body, called the lateral line. This detects movement and vibrations in the water.

7

GRAY REEF SHARK

Sometimes divers and snorkelers come face-to-face with one of the world's most threatening sharks—the gray reef shark. These hunters patrol coral reefs in groups.

Most sharks are **solitary** animals and live alone. Gray reef sharks, however, often swim in groups in quiet spots during the day. At night they go their separate ways to hunt. When a gray reef shark is feeling threatened it raises its snout, arches its back, and swims with a swaying motion. This menacing behavior warns enemies to move away—or prepare to be attacked.

Fishy Feasts

Gray reef sharks feed on squid, octopus, and small shelled animals such as shrimp and lobsters. They also prey on the colorful fish that live among the reefs, such as these beautiful butterfly fish.

SHARK BITES

HOW SCARY?

Length: Up to 8.5 ft (260 cm)

Habitat: Coral reefs

Where: Indian and Pacific Oceans

Weapons: Lots of friends, great agility, and 13–14 rows of teeth

ON THE MOVE

A pointed nose and a streamlined body help a shark to swim fast.

Moving through water is harder work than moving through air. Most fish have a **streamlined** body shape, which means their body moves through water easily. So fast swimmers usually have a long, slender shape.

Most sharks move quickly through water, and their bodies are packed with powerful muscles. The world's fastest shark is the shortfin mako. It is thought that this shark may reach speeds of 53 miles (88 kilometers) per hour—that's about the same speed as a cheetah chasing its **prey**.

Pectoral fins control direction and movements up and down.

The dorsal fin helps the fish to swim in S-shaped curves and stops it from rolling over.

The caudal, or tail, fin helps propel the shark through water.

KILLER FACT

Sharks have a big, oily liver that helps them to float, but if they stop swimming they sink to the seabed.

Slow Movers

Some sharks prefer life in the slow lane. They live on the seabed and move by swimming and almost "walking" with their fins. This leopard catshark roams the sandy seabed at night, searching for shellfish and small fish.

HAMMERHEAD SHARK

There are about 400 different types, or **species**, of shark and some of the strangest-looking ones are called hammerheads. Like its relatives—such as the mallethead sharks—the great hammerhead has an extraordinary appearance.

A hammerhead's nostrils are far apart, helping it to sense the direction of different smells.

A hammerhead's head is huge and wide, with eyes positioned right at the very ends. This shape probably helps the predator to move through water and change direction. The position of its eyes helps the shark to focus on its prey more easily, and work out how far away it is.

KILLER FACT

Hammerheads like to feast on venomous stingrays, and can even eat the venom-filled tails!

Fight for Life

Hammerheads can live for about 30 years, but few of them reach that great age. They are endangered, which means that they are at risk of becoming **extinct** because too many have been fished from the sea. They are also **cannibals**, and adults often prey on young hammerheads.

SHARK BITES

Length: Up to 20 ft (610 cm)

Habitat: Coastal waters and offshore

Where: Worldwide

Weapons: Good **binocular** vision and sharp teeth

HOW SCARY?

BASKING SHARK

The enormous mouth of a basking shark is large enough to hold a child. Fortunately, a basking shark has no interest in human prey because it only eats tiny plankton!

SHARK BITES

Length: Up to 39 ft (1,200 cm)

Habitat: Coasts and deep oceans

Where: Worldwide

Weapons: A VERY large mouth and sieve-like plates

The largest basking sharks weigh up to 21 tons (19 tonnes), five times as much as an elephant.

14

Water and plankton gush into the shark's huge gaping mouth.

Water passes out through the gill slits but the plankton is caught in the gills.

The huge slits on the side of a basking shark's head are called gill slits. Fish use **gills** instead of lungs to breathe underwater. Water, which contains oxygen, passes into their mouth and out through the gills. Basking sharks also use their gills to feed. Sieve-like plates in the gills trap any plankton in the water.

Actual size!

Plankton
Up to 3.2 in (8 cm)

KILLER FACT

Basking sharks often swim near the surface of the sea, and can even leap out of the water!

Mystery Shark

Sharks are mysterious creatures, and scientists need to find out much more about their lifestyles. It is known that basking sharks go on long journeys in spring and summer, but no one knows for sure where they disappear to from November to March.

GREAT WHITE SHARK

A great white's bite is three times more powerful than a lion's bite.

Does the great white shark really deserve to be called the oceans' most vicious predator? It is certainly well equipped to hunt, catch, and kill its prey.

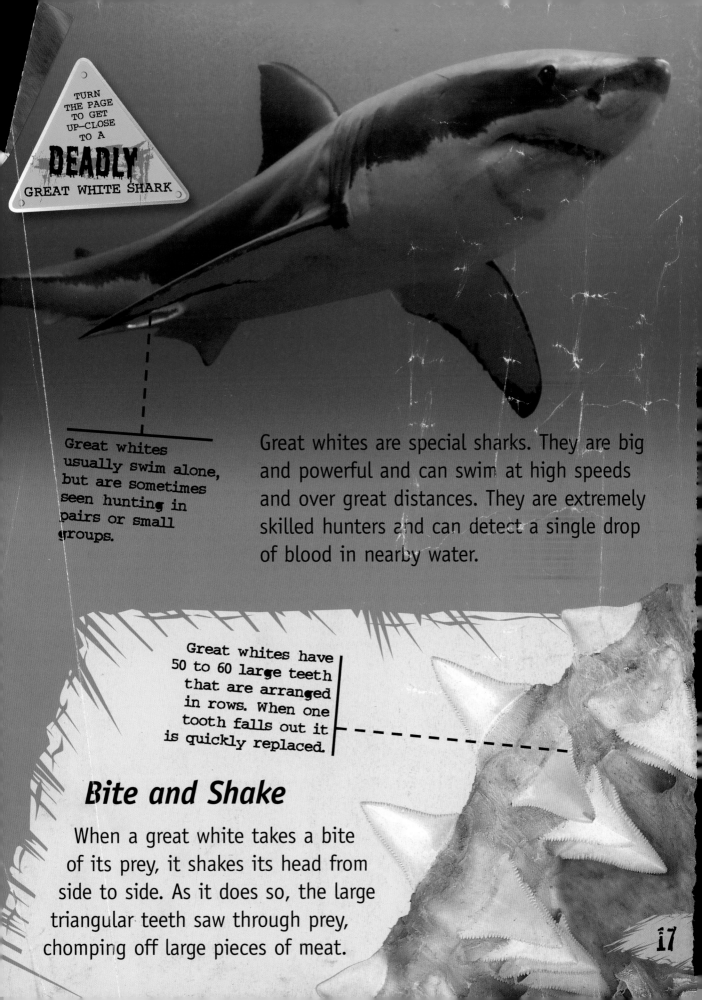

TURN
THE PAGE
TO GET
UP-CLOSE
TO A
DEADLY
GREAT WHITE SHARK

Great whites usually swim alone, but are sometimes seen hunting in pairs or small groups.

Great whites are special sharks. They are big and powerful and can swim at high speeds and over great distances. They are extremely skilled hunters and can detect a single drop of blood in nearby water.

Great whites have 50 to 60 large teeth that are arranged in rows. When one tooth falls out it is quickly replaced.

Bite and Shake

When a great white takes a bite of its prey, it shakes its head from side to side. As it does so, the large triangular teeth saw through prey, chomping off large pieces of meat.

SHARK BITES

Length: Up to 22 ft. (680 cm)

Habitat: Cool coastal waters and deep oceans

Where: Worldwide

Weapons: Powerful muscles, amazing speed, and a crunching bite

Actual size!

A great white shark's body is shaped like a torpedo. This allows it to move easily through the water. When it launches an attack, it can reach speeds of up to 15 mph (24 kph), powered along by its muscular tail. The sharks often attack their prey from underneath, so that the prey cannot see them coming.

TIGER SHARK

Meet the terrifying tiger shark—one of the most dangerous sharks in the world. These predators have been compared to garbage cans because they will try to eat almost anything.

They are called tiger sharks because their skin is marked with dark stripes and spots.

Tiger sharks are hungry, fearless hunters that come close to the shore in search of food. They spend most of the day slowly cruising through the water, but can suddenly burst into speed when they spy something tasty. They hunt sea turtles, clams, stingrays, sea snakes, seals, birds, and squid.

KILLER FACT

Tiger shark teeth are serrated, like a saw. As the shark bites, it throws its head from side to side, sawing through flesh.

SHARK BITES

Length: Up to 18 ft (550 cm)

Habitat: Coasts, reefs, harbors, and river mouths

Where: Warm tropical waters

Weapons: Replaceable teeth

HOW SCARY?

Scavengers

These sharks are **scavengers**, which means they are not fussy eaters and will feast on dead meat. Tiger sharks have been found with bottles, lumps of wood, potatoes, car tires—and even drums—in their stomachs!

21

SKELETONS AND SCALES

Most fish are bony fish. They have a bony skeleton that gives their body shape, power, and strength. Sharks, however, don't have bones. Instead, their skeleton is made from a strong, bendy material called **cartilage**.

KILLER FACT

It isn't just shark teeth that can hurt—their skin can, too. Its rough surface can tear the skin from a swimmer's leg.

Shark denticles

This swell shark has a spotted pattern to help it hide against the seabed.

Shark skin is covered with scales that are coated with enamel—the same tough material that makes our teeth hard. These scales are called **denticles**. Denticles help water to move smoothly over a shark, so it can swim fast.

Colors and Patterns

Some sharks have interesting patterns. Colors and patterns can help a shark to stay hidden from view. This is called **camouflage**. This wobbegong shark's strange shape and frilled mouth make a good disguise.

23

LEMON SHARK

Lemon sharks are large coastal sharks. They prefer to live in warm, shallow waters near land, especially during the day. At night they swim to deeper water.

Lemon sharks have wide, flat heads.

SHARK BITES

HOW SCARY?

Length: Up to 11 ft (340 cm)

Habitat: Reefs, mangroves, bays, and river mouths

Where: Warm American waters and West Africa

Weapons: Special electrical sensors and triangular teeth

Lemon sharks have small eyes and poor eyesight. The coastal waters where they live are often cloudy, so eyesight is not a great help in finding prey. Instead, these fish have special magnetic **sensors** in their snouts that help them find fish and shelled animals on the seabed.

Sharksuckers

Remoras, or sharksuckers, are long, thin fish with a special ability. They have suckers on the tops of their heads that they use to stick to a shark or other large fish and hitch a ride. They feed off any scraps that the shark does not eat.

Lemon sharks get their name from the yellow-brown color of their skin.

EGGS AND PUPS

Lemon sharks can give birth to as many as 17 pups in a single year.

Most fish lay eggs that hatch into baby fish. Sharks are special. Many of them don't lay eggs but give birth to their young instead. Young sharks are called **pups**.

Most mother sharks keep their pups inside their bodies while they grow. This means the pups are protected from predators for as long as possible. When the pups are born they are able to swim away. Sharks don't look after their pups.

Mermaid's Purse

Sharks that do lay eggs, such as catsharks, lay the eggs in a thick, rubbery case called a mermaid's purse. These egg cases often have curly strings, which attach them to rocks or seaweed to stop them from floating away. The shark pups grow inside for up to ten months.

Up to 3.2 in (8 cm)

Actual size!

This newborn lemon shark pup swims away from its mother.

KILLER FACT

Pups growing inside their mother may eat each other before they are even born. Sometimes only one or two pups survive.

LONGNOSE SAWSHARK

This small shark has a peculiar snout that makes up more than one quarter of its whole body length. The shark uses its strange nose, called a rostrum, as a lethal weapon and to detect prey.

The sides of the long nose are lined with rows of teeth.

Up to 17.6 in (45 cm)

Sawsharks have small, flat bodies because they live on the seabed and swim close to the bottom, where they hunt for small fish, squid, and shrimp. The long nose is called a saw and is lined with long, sharp teeth. Long feelers on the saw, called barbels, are used for touch. Sawsharks also have teeth in their jaws, which they use for biting.

As they cruise along the seabed, sawsharks use their barbels to detect prey hidden in the sand and mud.

SHARK BITES

Length: Up to 4.6 ft (140 cm)

Habitat: Seabed in coastal areas

Where: Southern Australia

Weapons: Sensitive detectors and small, needle-sharp teeth

KILLER FACT

Sawsharks sense electricity using organs called ampullae of Lorenzini. These are small, gel-filled holes in their saw.

Electric Sense

These sharks use their saw to swipe at their prey, or to rake through mud and dislodge animals hiding there. Their saw has another great use—it can detect electricity. All animals use electricity to make their muscles work, and sharks have a super-sense that helps them to detect it.

SHARKS AND PEOPLE

Humans are much more deadly than sharks. It is rare for sharks to attack people, and most of those human victims do survive an attack. People, however, kill up to 120 million sharks every year.

Many of these majestic marine predators are now in grave danger of becoming **extinct**. That means they may disappear from our planet forever. Sharks are fished from the seas for their meat and their fins, which are used in soup. They are also caught accidentally by fishermen who are hoping to catch other fish to eat.

This dogfish died after getting tangled in a fisherman's net.

Shark cages allow scientists to study sharks close-up, without either the divers or the sharks getting into trouble.

Saving Sharks

We need sharks in our seas. They are part of the ocean ecosystem, and they play an important part in keeping the oceans healthy and in balance. We can help by not buying shark products, and by learning as much as we can about these beautiful fish.

KILLER FACT

There used to be ten times as many sharks in the oceans as there are today.

GLOSSARY

binocular
Seeing using both eyes together. Binocular vision is good for hunting.

camouflage
A pattern of colors and/or shapes on an animal's body that hides it from predators or prey.

cannibals
Animals that eat others from the same species.

cartilage
A strong, flexible fiber in animals' bodies. Sharks' skeletons are made from cartilage.

denticles
Hard scales on a shark's skin that help streamline the shark's body.

extinct
A species of animal that is no longer alive.

freshwater
Water without salt in it, such as that found in rivers and most lakes.

gills
Organs used by fish to breathe. The gills collect oxygen that is dissolved in the water.

plankton
Small animals and plants that float in the oceans, carried along by the ocean currents.

predators
Animals that hunt other animals to eat.

prey
Animals that are hunted by predators.

pup
The young of a shark.

scavenger
An animal that feeds on dead animals or plants that it finds. Some sharks are scavengers.

sensors
Organs in an animal that respond to stimuli such as light or magnetism.

solitary
Living alone, away from other members of the same species.

species
A kind of animal or plant. Members of the same species are able to breed, producing young.

streamlined
A smooth shape that allows fluids such as water to flow easily around it.

TAKING IT FURTHER

What makes a shark "scary"? Now it's time for you to decide.

- Choose some scary features, such as speed, size, habitat, aggressive personality, and favorite food.

- Use this book, and the Internet, to award up to five points for each of a shark's scary features. Repeat for as many sharks as you want.

- Turn your results into a table, graph, or chart. Add up the totals to get a "Scary Score" for each type of shark.

USEFUL WEBSITES

www.sharktrust.org
Discover more about the interesting world of sharks.

www.flmnh.ufl.edu/fish/sharks
A great website for finding up-to-date information on sharks.

ocean.nationalgeographic.com/ocean
For facts and photos about sharks and their habitat.

www.arkive.org
Essential information on endangered animals, including sharks.

TOP 5 DEADLY SHARK FACTS!

Sharks can see in dark water, but they are probably color-blind.

One big meal is enough to keep some sharks alive for many months.

Sharks lose thousands of teeth over a lifetime, but new ones replace them.

There are nearly 400 different species of shark, but only about 12 of them are dangerous to humans.

The smallest shark in the world, the dwarf lanternshark, grows to just 8 inches (20 centimeters) long.

INDEX

ampullae of Lorenzini 29

barbels 28
basking shark 14–15
biting 17, 20, 28
blue shark 5
breathing 15
bull shark 6–7

camouflage 23
cannibals 13, 27
cartilage 22
catsharks 11, 27
caudal fin 11
coastal sharks 6, 20, 24
coral reefs 8, 9

denticles 23
dogfish 30
dorsal fin 11
dwarf lanternshark 33

eggs 26, 27
electricity 29
enamel 23
endangered species 13, 30
extinction 13, 30
eyesight 5, 7, 24, 33

fins 10, 11
fishing 13, 30
food 4, 5, 9, 12, 14,
   20, 21, 33

freshwater 6
frilled shark 4

gills 15
gray reef shark 8–9
great hammerhead 12
great white shark 16–17

hammerhead shark 12–13
humans 4, 5, 30–31

lateral line 7
lemon shark 24–25, 26
leopard catshark 11
liver 11
longnose sawshark 28–29

magnetic sensors 24
mallethead shark 12
mermaid's purse 27
mouth 14, 23
movement 10–11
muscles 10, 29

nostrils 12

oceans 31

patterns 20, 23
pectoral fins 10
plankton 4, 14, 15
predators 4, 16, 20
pups 26, 27

reef sharks 8-9
remoras 25

sawsharks 28–29
scales 23
scavengers 21
seabed 11, 28
senses 7, 29
sensors 24
shape 10, 19, 28
shark cages 31
sharksuckers 25
shortfin mako 10
size 4, 14, 33
skeleton 22
skin 22, 23
smell, sense of 7, 12
snout 5, 10, 24, 28
solitary sharks 6, 8
species 12
speed 4, 10, 17, 19, 20, 23
streamlining 10, 19
swell shark 23
swimming 10–11, 17, 23

teeth 4, 17, 20, 28, 33
territories 8
tiger shark 20–21
touch 28

vision 5, 7, 12, 24, 33

whale shark 4
wobbegong shark 23